About the author

I met the author of this book, Heikki Nousiainen, in the beginning of the nineties, when we both trained Kyukushinkai karate. I trained this style under couple of years as an extra training to my own karatestyle, Motobu-ha Shitoryu. I had started my training in the age of twelve.

Heikki has been working with many different martial arts such as Tai Chi, which he has taught, as a professional martial artist, for the longest period of time. He has also studied and instructed in many different Chinese martial arts as well as martial arts from Philippines and even other South-East Asian martial arts. I have studied Chinese martial arts under his guidance.

We have exchanged knowledge about martial arts from the beginning of the nineties and we also have become good friends, above our shared interest in the world of martial arts.

Heikki is a professional teacher who has trained the most of the martial arts still existing today. He has also worked in many of them more deeply and he has got the possibility to train the fine parts of different arts and the special techniques of these arts.

I wish him the best of luck with the book. I think it is good that he shares his knowledge and it is something he should continue to do. Our joined venture will continue also for many years to come, this is my

sincerely hope at least.

Fight greetings

Renshi Johan Backteman

6.dan Motobu-ha shitoryu karate-do,

Goshindo, Kobudo, Iaido

Heikki

I met Heikki for the first time in Stockholm. We were both attending William C. Chens Tai Chi seminar 1990. We learned to know each other training self-defense applications of Tai Chi. Heikki invited me to come to Umeå and have a training camp at his dojo/gym.

This was the beginning of a joined venture among martial arts that has lasted for years. I was staying at Heikkis home and we exchanged our views about fighting. Heikki visited Turku to attend seminars and he also taught Chinese martial arts in Turku. I changed my style of tai chi from Yang to Wudang because I liked its approach and its focus on the martial side of the art. I suggested Heikki to check this style and the European head coach Dan Docherty. Heikki was as always interested and open for new things, so for this practical Tai Chi also. He started to train the syllabus and its secrets with great intensity.

I sometimes envy Heikki his capacity to get so excited and to put all his effort in new things, I, myself, am very slow to start to like every kind of changes and I really could not keep up to Heikkis tempo. Heikki has also travelled a lot around the world to be able to train different martial arts. He is familiar with many styles and is always eager to learn new things.

Seen in the retrospective he has done a great carrier among martial arts and it is also great that he can share his knowledge and teaching by writing.

Tommi Halsvaha is born 1958 and has been a practitioner and teacher in Turku Finland. He has 3 dan black belt in Yushinkai karatejutsu and Ryukyu kempo and he has been training tai chi under many years. Tommi started a karate and tai chi association in Kaarina 1992 which is still active. Tommi Halsvaha is also known as a teacher in social and health care institutions and schools. He is teaching Controlled Physical Restriction, which is a system planned and formed for personal working within social and health care. The aim or goal of the system is to restrict safely and without, or so little pain, as possible, un aggressive person, not to forget verbal and non-verbal communication. Halsvaha has a special level of psychotherapy education and he has a license to teach relaxation and hypnosis.

Tommi Halsvaha

Foreword

This is the first book in English about the method/methods of pushing hands, used in the martial art of tai chi chuan (taiji), that covers the many aspects of the phenomena. It is not meant to be a teaching tool, as my first book about tai chi was, but a deeper analysis what pushing hands is, why you practice it and what is its role in the art of tai chi.

When I started to practice tai chi more than thirty years ago, pushing hands or tui shou usually was referred in tai chi books as a secret and mysterious method only reserved the very advanced hard core practitioners. I hope that this book can clarify and make sense of this method of practice. It is actually only an aid, tool of practice, although very functional and intelligent way to practice the things needed in tai chi and in self-defense in general. I will in this book use PH instead of pushing hands.

One of my goals as a tai chi teacher has been to unclothe the mysterious coverage over the phenomena of tai chi chuan without making things too simple. I want not that the complexity and many aspects of tai chi should be left away. Tai chi is so complicated and interesting phenomena that it does not need beautiful words to be exotic, esoteric and very exciting. In the matter of fact it is an art and to master it and its theory does need effort and time. As my late Chinese Kung Fu teacher, Lawrence Leong (1940-1999) often repeated the saying, "Kung Fu is easy to learn but hard to master". I would like to say as -if acting in theater- oh so true, so true. When I started to practice tai chi as a very young but self-confident, self-secure person I was sure that I could in somehow solve the problem or phenomena called tai chi. I collected all the newspaper articles, University studies and papers written about tai chi, all the books in the market at that time in English, Finnish, Swedish and

Germany (although my Germany is not so good), even French books about tai chi. After reading all the material I noticed that it was not the right way. I left the books for many years and concentrated in training.

This is my second book I have written about tai chi. The first one includes no tai chi theory, not hardly any text to mention. It is the tai chi hand form shown with photos that makes it possible to study it on your own. I want in my books to follow the same path that the tai chi classics recommend; first comes practice or "doing", after that comes analysis and reflection. This book starts to handle with tai chi theory and tai chi classics, especially concerning the strategy and tactics of close quarter combat needed in PH.

My goal is to dig deeper and deeper in tai chi theory book by book, until there is only simple doing left, in that way we have closed the circle and have come back to unity.

I hope that I have been able to clarify the concept of PH both for beginners and advanced students. Only the reader can decide whether or not I have succeeded. I also hope that the reader will follow the recommendation of tai chi chuan classics " just do it" and practice well and not only in an armchair. This being said I hope you will have enjoyable moments with this book in the armchair!

Introduction

I still remember the feeling, excited curiosity and eagerness, when I read about a course in tai chi for beginners on the information wall in library more than thirty years ago. An old, ancient martial art that combined philosophy, health, meditation and combat. I could not imagine any other subject that was so interesting and fascinating and it still is. My interest and passion for the art are still there although there had been doubts, even worse things about after every decade that has passed by but I do not worry about that. In a good relationship it is only natural to have and express even negative feelings. I think that it is your duty to question your doings every now and then, people change and so do situations and it is not good to end up in a situation you do something you do not like. You will not be comfortable and if you are a professional teacher in tai chi, people will notice it. It is totally another thing to feel the desire not to train just like at this moment I am writing this book in Catania, Sicily. Outside there is beautiful weather and all the sounds and exciting odors of food etc. I have decided to do my Nei Kung (Internal strength) exercises after I finish writing and then go out. I feel that I could do without training BUT I know also that I will enjoy more my outgoing after exercising. I am more relaxed and open for what I will see and experience today. Training should although not become something like a heavy back bag you carry around, on the contrary it should be something you get more energy and joy of. More about this subject (the art of joy in training) in oncoming books, it is important!

My first tai chi teacher was a Chinese man, who was an artistic person, a great musician as well. He weighted little, only 46 kg and he did the tai chi hand form so well that I will never reach that level or at least not the artistic expression. It is good someone sets the standard that high so you have to always try to improve. He had been trained since three years age. His base was tremendously strong, a proof of the hard training as a kid he had got a muscle that grew over his shinbone protecting that. I did not believe that before I got the possibility to see and touch the muscle myself, there was a muscle! Unfortunately the hard training had efficiently killed the joy of training and the enthusiasm for the art. He told me that he is only teaching and training for money although the image he gave the people was the opposite. He even told me that people are not searching for a teacher but a guru and a father and he used this fact skillfully, as well as the image to be a mysterious china man with modern thoughts. He considered people to be too lazy to learn PH, self-defense, weapons of tai chi or the more heavy training which is also quite often monotonous, even boring from time to time. This is partly why I want to teach people to become their own instructors and I will start to teach PH, self-defense from day one. When a new tai chi book was published by a lady who had been a member of a Olympic team in gymnastic, with her ability to make really nice tai chi postures because of the flexibility training in gymnastics, my teachers comment was that it was not tai chi. It is not enough to have a superior capabilities in your body, that is true. It is first in movement you see the quality of each person's tai chi. The level of tai chi can be bad though the person has all the physical attributes needed. The lady did perfect postures, it was a fact but he did not want to see it. This attitude is unfortunately quite common in martial arts, only you and your instructor are capable, the rest are faking something. In my mind every instructor has something to give if you listen. Even of the bad things you can learn but please, do not repeat or copy your teacher's bad habits, everyone has got them. It is no use to spend all your time to search for a perfect teacher. There is though a point to try to find a good teacher for you.

My teacher noticed my eager to learn and he sent me to Asia to get that knowledge. I will always be grateful for that to my teacher and also for the fact that he showed me the beginning of a long path of martial arts. He was also skillful, at that time 99 percent of tai chi teachers would not have been near his level. I was lucky to have him as a teacher although I am a bit critical also. It was also a bit comical when we senior students asked when we could start to learn that and that and the answer was always after ten years. We calculated that we would end up being at least 200 years old before we can the whole system.....I think a martial system should be possible to learn in a quite short time if you put all your effort in it. Think about Chinese or Indian restaurant that have hundreds of different courses on their menu. Do You think that You get fresh local produced food? I prefer a restaurant that has one or maximum three meals on their menu.

This is maybe beyond the frame of this book but of course a martial arts teacher must have also an academic interest in his/her own martial art, which means that he/she studies different arts and his own in depth but pay attention to this; nobody can have fresh knowledge about everything. The old masters used a lot of time to FORGET the patterns and drills they trained for years, in order not to become slaves under a system.

So, I am still on my way to new experiences, maybe the experiences nowadays happens more in my own body and mind. I still travel a lot to learn and teach martial arts. I have always been happy to take part of new beginner´s courses in different arts but because my physical level is not the same anymore I prefer private lessons or seminars nowadays.

I met a Finnish tai chi and karate teacher from Turku in Sweden, Stockholm. We were at a seminar with William C Chen, maybe the teacher who at that time was most famous in the world. I will tell you more about Tommi in my later books but for now he was the one who told me about a teacher who had said in Combat magazine that the most tai chi teachers cannot use their art for fighting and so especially the ones who belong Yang family tai chi. I got very curious and called him to London and I dared to question his teachings. It was only his words, I could not know if he walks the walk. The teacher, Dan Docherty, made an offer. I could come to London and pay the same amount for his teaching what I charged for my own private students and If I was not satisfied after an week I would get all my money back. I travelled to London and I did not have to use my option. My teacher had newly moved from Hong Kong to London so he wanted to make a difference and he did. Actually the most of my knowledge in PH and especially in tai chi theory and classics comes from him. I have though done my homework and research even on my own like everybody else needs to do. My motto is: become your own teacher. When I have finished my work with teaching I am unemployed, many teachers, especially teachers from and in Asia want to bind their students with their own person and school. My point is that in martial arts you are always alone, if a bad situation should happen, you better develop your own thinking and ability to solve a difficult situation or even defend yourself, your teacher will not be there to give the right answer.

What is pushing hands

It is easier to come more near a good answer to that question by defining what PH is not. PH is not a mystical, exotic or esoteric capability or attribute you can achieve by meditating. For a beginner it might even seem to be somewhat mystical the easiness when an advanced practitioner of tai chi can neutralize the opponent's trials to attack and unbalance a beginner. It seems and even feels (if you are on close quarter and in contact) that the more experienced person can anticipate and knows in advantage what the opponent tries to do. This is exactly what also happens in PH. A skillful tai chi practitioner feels the opponents attacks a little bit before so that he/she can easily and without the use of force neutralize his/her opponents attempts. He can also choose to unbalance his opponent or use other options depending on the situation, locking, breaking, hitting, kicking, throwing, sweeping etc.

The skill is not coming to you from heaven, it is based on hundreds and hundreds, thousands of hours of practice with so many people as possible. It is an ability everyone gets by training. It is the same thing as a skillful judoka (a person who practices judo) or jujutsuka can play with a beginner using no force at all to mention. In tai chi many methods and exercises are formalized and have different rules you have to obey which makes the advantage to the people familiar with the system even greater. The rules are there to make the training safe and/or to concentrate on certain aspects of the art that are important to improve to become a well-rounded healthy tai chi man or a woman. These attributes are for example good posture, good balance and coordination, timing, the use of the whole body as a unit etc.

Some of the methods used in PH are Chinese wrestling and not really "pure" PH. In this context it is good to remember that in tai chi we normally are defending ourselves against multiple opponents. This means that wrestling standing or on the ground is not an option, it is suicide. Even though in some PH methods you are not allowed to take steps, your self-defense is based on mobility and how you place your own body depending of your opponent's position. It is not an easy task to neutralize an attack and try to do it in a way that you can use the attacker as a shield, or sweep him in a way that he lands between you and the next opponent, or throw, push him in that manner, at the same time you should have the most advantageous place against the rest of the opponents.

In this book we will dig deeper what PH really is all about but already we can make a statement that it is really only a teaching tool when we learn self-defense. With the help of PH we can gain the tenth of a second, when our opponent is unbalanced and we are in good balance and can attack with full force. To continue our list what PH is not we can see that it is not wrestling nor pure self-defense. We could take up, in this context, the critics against PH competitions that are regularly coming up in the tai chi world. Two things are true, nobody wants to start to do PH in the street, it is also true that with very free rules there is the necessity to use force. Believe me; it will happen in the street as well. It is very rare in a real combat that somebody is so superior technically that he or she can manage without using force. Naturally our ambition is to refine our skills and use so little effort and force as possible. Instead of power or force we should maybe talk about trained force or explosive force. Tai chi without force would be empty or none existing, even according to the tai chi classics. We come back to this subject already in this book. The question is not force or not force; it is force or power versus trained force or explosive force or energy.

Competition can be considered as a good test but more about this later, in the chapter about competition and its be or not to be.

I consider PH, above being an excellent training method and aid, as something that makes tai chi different from other martial arts. In every Asian martial art you strive after a relaxed way to perform and to use an opponents strength against himself.

Slow movements and training methods are to be found in many systems, also circular movements, the use of the whole body as a unit etc. but only tai chi has pushing hands or tui shou.

I have trained many systems that has methods that reminds PH and they have at least partly the same goal as tai chi. I have trained in four different schools of Wing Chun (Sorry if somebody thinks this is wrongly spelled, there are many ways and this is not meant as a statement in any way) and they have for example chi sau. Filipino Kali has also methods similar PH as well as Silat, even Gojuryu karate has similar methods as PH practiced on a higher level, what I know.

I have no right to say that above is true because I do not know the systems well enough to make a precise analysis. I can only mention that even though tai chi's PH is unique it is not so that only tai chi has invented this kind of training methods. My point is that even that same type of training systems exist in other systems so in my mind PH makes tai chi real and unique.

Summa summarum : We have so far come to two conclusions what PH is. It is a very important and intelligent working tool, which helps us train things needed in self-defense, the same applies for the health, correct use of the body improves also health aspects. This is true in every aspect of tai chi but is not the focus of this book. It is also an unique method which is almost like a trademark for tai chi.

Slow, relaxed movements are not a goal in itself. It is a way to extreme speed. Everybody can make a test with their hand speed, first by tensing all the muscles in the arm and trying to hit fast, then relaxing as much as possible and then hitting. The relaxation is common in every martial art, maybe tai chi has more focus on it, maybe we focus on it too much or in a wrong way. It has nothing to do for example with a bad, collapsed posture as a result trying to relax too much. Many top athletes look very relaxed and even have laziness in their style. I think about the best high jumper in the world (he has still the world record) Patrik Sjöberg when he was still competing. He used to smoke behind the competition scene and looked like a drug addict but I know people who have lifted weights with him and they were ashamed when this skinny guy was superior muscular, well trained men in many different exercises and it was not only leg muscles. I think it is obvious that there can be no explosion without power. Also in tai chi it is question of relaxed, explosive power/force. The difference between high jump and tai chi is that the time and space is much more limited in tai chi. The explosion should be done with so little movement that you hardly can see it.

I think that it should be clear by now that PH is not only, as the name states, pushing each other's hands in a friendly manner. You can train a lot of attributes or skills depending which kind of PH exercise you are doing. One thing is common with all the exercises and it is that we do have contact with our training partner, hands are almost all the time in contact too, or they should be. We are going to take a more near look at these skills trained by looking at different exercises designed to different purposes.

What do the tai chi chuan classics say?

Tai chi classics creates the base or theoretical background of tai chi. The texts do not necessarily open and make sense even after several years of actually study of the art of tai chi chuan. The classics need interpretation. I have been reading translations of classics where you quite soon realize that the author has not got enough knowledge of the art of tai chi or his or her language skills are not adequate. To make sense of tai chi classics there are three conditions that has to be fulfilled. The authors own knowledge of the art of tai chi has to be on a high level, his or her knowledge in Chinese language and in the language the translation is done, both languages have to be on a high level, last but not least his or her writing skills have to be on a extraordinary level so that complicated things can be expressed in a way that the reader will understand. There is at least one tai chi teacher that has what these requirements demand, Dan Docherty. According to himself, the two mentioned requirements has to be fulfilled but my point is that all three has to be in harmony. This can result in a coherent body of text/ texts that can be understood not only by experts but even by a bigger audience.

In the middle of nineties many of my best students were University teachers or studied philosophy at University level. I was teaching them all tai chi as a martial art, not as a health exercise. With these people we formed a group where we discussed tai chi classics, tai chi theory, history and philosophy and translations between different languages. The group attended tai chi training three, four times a week, many in the group took also private lessons from me and almost all trained daily at home. The discussions took place above all this training so the most were really qualified to leave their contribution. We did have good time too. I believe that we could help Dan Docherty with one word, concerning translations of important terminology. It may seem to be a very poor result of so many intelligent and well educated people but the reader has to remember that none of us had English or Chinese as their mother language. We did get results for our own understanding and we were feeling good about training hard and even reflecting what we were doing. We were playing tai chi, with it I mean exploring, not only following the great master but seeking the same things that the masters were seeking, using their knowledge as a guide and home base. At the same time I was teaching tai chi on many different levels. I had even so called special groups, they could be professional football players or disabled. I had also a special group with restricted capability to see, many of them were simply blind. It was obvious that PH exercises worked best in this group because they all had developed the sense to feel!

The grandmaster, Cheng Tin- Hung had to memorize all the classics while doing Nei Kung exercises. That is a tremendous task but maybe memorizing the classics helped in fact doing the demanding Nei Kung exercises, not the other way round. I have always used extra tasks when students do basic stance training. Everyone can try this. Try to stay in a deep horse stance ,measure the time carefully. The next day or day after you do the same but give to yourself different tasks. For example train to punch, not like a mad man but train details or some type of hitting you are not so familiar with. With a partner this is easier, one is hitting and one parrying in different ways. I think 100% of you that made this test improved their time quite considerably when doing extra things while trying to hold a demanding posture.

Tai chi classics are made by five different texts but which contain repetition and the level of writing also varies as well as the motives. I will come back to the classics in later volumes but in this context I will only take up a couple of important concepts, which we were discussing in the group I mentioned. The group was functioning under many years so we had time to do a lot of thinking. To get a deeper presentation you can read Dan Dochertys own translations of classics and his interpretations of the same classics.

"If your technique is broken, the intent is not broken"

This sentence, saying or core of truth is expressed in two different places in the classics. It is of utmost importance both in PH as well as in self-defense. It means that the technique we have tried to apply is not successful or we fail to fulfill it, so our intent to carry on is not broken and swiftly and fast we try another technique without any interruption and delay.

In more free exercises as well as in a real situation we can not count on that we manage to do everything we intent to but our intention and determination to fulfill our task will not change. For example a dog which misses its bite does not stop but naturally continues its attack and stops when the situation is clear, defeat or victory. Of course we have to assume that our opponent has the same determination as we do.

"Four grams can displace 1000 kg".

The reader can imagine a wheel that is coming to us with high speed, we only need to give it a little push to the side to make it to change its direction. This is basically what we try to do in tai chi. We use softness to overcome hardness. We are not blocking a punch but redirect it to emptiness by using footwork and /or twisting the waist and hips.

This is the second claim that is present at two different places in the classics. It indicates that is is of a key value. One of my teachers used to say that if some technique was present in several of the arts he was teaching it was time to think that maybe it was an importat one, worth of a closer look. The techniques have been changing and evolving so long time so that if there is the one and same technique in different arts you should take them seriously. The student has although the responsibility to test everything themselves, because not every technique is working for everybody. Even according to the scientific study of training and its effects on human body is known that the best training methods has a population of 4 procent that it will not affect their results

We struggled once with a martial application of single whip. We could not get it working properly and the only thing we learned was that a taller person can do it to a smaller person but not vice versa. This was confirmed by our teacher in next international meeting.

Everybody is responsible to study techniques she or he learns and of them choose her or his favorite ones. It has everything to do with weight, length, power, skill and personal preferences.

There is also a saying that how can an old man defend himself against several younger opponents.

This can be seen as a symbolic way of expressing the fact that softness and relaxation are important, not necessarily to say that an eighty years old man can successfully defend against a group of people.

One of the PH exercises is referring direct to tai chi classics. In the exercise we are dealing with powers which formed the old name of tai chi, 13 tactics. The name refers to eight forces and five ways to move.

We are only explaining the four powers which the exercise is referring to.

According to The classics: " Peng, lu ,ji, an must be taken seriously. Up and down follow each other and our opponent cannot reach us. Let him attack with force, use four grams to move 1000 kg". Peng is a force directed upwards, lu is directing the force to the side, an is pushing downwards and li is push straight forward.

Chinese like numbers and they use them skillfully. The message hidden in the classics, the complexity and sometimes even stupid complexity, makes things difficult for a dedicated discipline of tai chi chuan.

In the long run and especially when your hobby has become a lifelong interest can it be interesting that there are so many levels in tai chi. When I lecture about tai chi I often claim that one should know all the different sciences there are in order to be able to explain the phenomena called tai chi chuan. This might be the case with every phenomena of some complexity?

The Tai Chi Classics do not open and reveal their secrets easily. I therefore recommend listening to them at the same time you do your Nei Kung exercises. I have used this method myself. Dan Docherty has made a CD where the classics are clearly pronounced in English, Chinese and French. The texts are not necessarily easier to understand on your own language but why not to make an effort to translate, during the process you sure will learn something and at least you end up with a lot of interesting questions.

The classics are like foreign languages, very difficult in the beginning but if you put in the effort needed, new world will open up and new ways of interpreting the world you only had one way to interpret. At the same way studying becomes more interesting the more you know, the work or study becomes exploring, researching and you will have fun while you are doing it.

The tai chi classics recommend to do things and there are already enough armchair teachers as my teacher calls them in one of his books. Training first, reflection later. To listen to classics while doing Nei Kung is to recommend, maybe you find out that it makes Nei Kung easier or more meaningful to do. Nei kung in itself is the foundation that for example makes our PH and self-defense to work.

The most important quality; listening

Listening is without a doubt the most important attribute in PH. To be able to listen we have to be relaxed. Relaxation as a concept that creates confusion. Relaxation in this context does not mean that we somehow are totally without any willpower and intention and almost fall down on the floor like an empty paper bag, although there is also an exercise that we train that quality too.

Especially when Chinese teachers want to see relaxation the above mentioned happens, people become like wax you can form.

This is not the meaning, it is to be able to relax, be soft, yin so that we can listen where does our opponents force come from, when and with how much power and which way is it heading. We need this ability to listen in order to redirect the force to the side and after that we can attack with appropriate force and technique, depending on the situation.

It is a process that contains three different parts, relaxation makes the two first possible and actually even the third one, because trained or explosive power cannot exist without relaxation and softness as a precondition to it.

In this book we deal with some important theoretical concepts but we still have wanted to keep them as few as possible, in oncoming books we are diving more deep in to the theory, tai chi classics, history and basic concepts compared this volume. This is done partly of the obvious reason NOT to get lost in theory; the practical side of PH maybe also diminishes if we deal too much with cryptically sayings in the tai chi classics.

My point is that through practical exercises one can achieve understanding of the strategies of close combat. One of them is to control our opponents hands, have continuity in our techniques, softness which make listening possible, redirecting the force to the side and the use of trained or explosive energy, to follow, continuous contact and to avoid brute force.

Practical exercises help to understand different strategies and by doing exercises you get a deeper understanding of the whole art and it is not only words by which you can make an impression to people. In the beginning.........in the same way there was in tai chi and PH the exercises and techniques first, reflection and theory came in the picture later on.

Are PH competitions bad for the art of tai chi chuan?

This question or a claim that they definitely are bad is always present among tai chi teachers. I think it is a valid question whether or not there should be competitions but to answer that question in a simplistic way, yes or no, is hardly possible.

If You look at the competitions from a philosophical point of view competition in PH, tai chi or competition in general is not healthy nor a wise thing to do.

In sport in general you are always in hurry and even though you are in nature for example running, so you do not have time to see the nature or view. Your focus is on your watch, pulse meter and other equipment to measure different things.

Athletes do make even their body to a thing, quite often they tell after competition, " I could not get more power from the engine", that is their own body.

In China young kids have to specialize, for example, in tai chi form which is not good for them or for the art itself.

I met once people in a tai chi competition in Denmark. They claimed that they were tai chi people but did only compete in PH. Not one of them did compete in forms, san shou (kicks, throws, punches etc allowed) competition was not included in that competition.

Their best representative told me that he had ten years experience in wrestling.

I think you should train your art as a whole, all the aspects, otherwise you and your art become more restricted, you are more vulnerable for sports injuries etc. The question is if you are highly specialized, is it longer tai chi you are practicing? If ice hockey would be a game where you hold hands, smile and look good, would that be ice hockey anymore?

One argument is that competitions result in brute force between young men. Well, try to always manage a self-defense situation without force, if you can your ability is very high, the rest of us must quite often use it and only, almost accidentally can manage with only refined techniques.

One of the main arguments FOR competitions is just the fact that young men can test their skills and force, if you want, under certain rules without so big risk for serious injury. The second good thing is that it is a good pressure test which tells you something about your own level of tai chi. You do not meet a drunk in a street (not said that it is easy) but a sober person who has been prepared for a competition, trained hard for a long time and can a lot of same techniques as you can or more or better. He is not your friend or training partner either. He wants to win. Competition is not for everyone but it is good to try if you dare. One of my students was always very good at competitions, even though he was lazy in training situations, that is an exception, the most people start to train hard if they compete, because nobody wants to lose his face. The dark side of this is that even talented people stop training after they stop competing. They need the adrenalin kicks and medals and when that is not present, they are not motivated to continue. To compete and make the reparations for that can in its best teach people mental training that they can use in other fields of life. Local small competition can be goals on a lower level, then national and finally international competition, maybe the championship of Europe as the biggest goal. Arguments against and for competition are legion. I am in one sense against competitions but all the people I have met in competitions train hard and for me personally, it was important to find out that I can take the pressure before competitions and even win. I cannot believe that there is anything bad with that.

Maybe one negative thing was that after finished competing, at least I, had a bad consciousness that I was training too little number of hours per week. It took some time to find a new equilibrium. One of my college, when I was a professional masseur, told me that when the doctor told him that he cannot compete in tae-kwon-do any more, he started to cry and eat medicine, went up 50 kg in one year. Here the question is that there should be a plan how you deactivate or stop your career as a competition athlete. The case I mentioned went well, the guy made the kilos in to muscles and got over with his depression but sometimes things do not go so well.

One friend of mine who was a boxer on a high level said that nobody cares about the athletes after they stop producing medals. That is true and although competition in tai chi is not on that level it might be true some day.

The ex top athletes should train young people and the problem even in martial arts is that if the best guys get problems after their career with criminality, drugs etc, the parents won't let their children begin classes in martial arts.

I think it is also good to test how your own techniques bite against people in your own art. As one guy in Holland who lost against me in a competition was so frustrated that he tried to kick me several times in the groin when he lost points and balance. His family, girlfriend, the whole team was watching him to lose and he had planned to win over this old man and he found himself on the matt time after time. A pressure test is good if you put it in right light so to say. Do not value winning in competitions too high. Do not be blinded with competing.

Some teachers believe that every kind of sparring, full contact matches, PH competitions are bad for your overall capability to defend yourself. I understand that they are two different things but when you give competition right place and time it can not be bad for you, it is actually good for you, especially if you can go and take a beer with the guys afterwards.

Why do we have PH drills?

PH drills have naturally developed to serve goals that a martial art has, the main one is to improve one's capability to defend oneself even against several opponents which might have weapons or not. Likewise in every other martial art this capability is based on certain attributes or skills which we train with PH drills. The main philosophy "behind" tai chi is Taoism, so the idea of balance, health and moderate way of doing things is present. Maybe this is one of the reasons in many people's minds tai chi is an health exercise only. This is not bad in itself; there is a wide variety of different exercise systems nowadays based on boxing or other martial arts. The problem with tai chi is that the original meaning and skill is diminishing. Nobody is mixing condition boxing with real boxing, with tai chi this has happened. Above this many of the more demanding drills or ways to drill that are demanding have been forgotten. It is always sad if any kind of art form and its tradition is shrinking.

What qualities are trained in PH?

From discussions above the reader should by now understand that in PH you do also something else than only push with your hands at random. Above coordination and balance partner drills teach the practitioner footwork, timing and distance. Other benefits are that we have time to correct the right position of knee and feet, the use of waist and hips and last but not least, overall body mechanics. Good body mechanics help you to avoid injuries and you improve your balance, body position and correct posture and to use your whole body as a unit to gain maximum power.

The most important quality that we improve by PH drills is listening. By being in contact with our training partner we learn to listen with our body, according to the classics we listen how much power, from where, where it is heading and after that we learn how to redirect it to emptiness.

We are coming back to tai chi theory and tai chi classics because they are central when we talk about PH drills. To be able to listen other peoples energies does not only take a lot fo time but it is important to listen to many different kinds of energies. We have to train with so many people as possible and so our improvement is depending, in a way, on other people. Without our training partners we cannot improve.

The basic muscle tonus is different with everyone, different people have different skills and training backgrounds which affects their ability to use power etc. Only by training with many partners we can reach our own maximum potential. Above it, it is great fun and we surely get surprised every now and then.

This is maybe the big tai chi event in France uses afternoons for pushing hands. Every tenth minute you seek a new partner, hopefully you are polite and ask at which level he or she wants to train and then you do it. Complete beginners can meet the champion of Europe in PH or a teacher with more than 30 years' experience of tai chi. I have seen how younger guys go for it and are totally exhausted after first ten minutes, elderly people maybe do It more like a gentle drill etc. I think you should use the time for listening even if you are willing to train harder, try to listen and neutralize, of course some people are so gentle that they do nothing.

In my own groups I use role play. I want extremely fit and advanced people only to neutralize and shy or what could we call them, people who do not want to attack, to attack all the time. It is waste of time doing PH without intention to unbalance your training partner. I recommend dancing but even there you have to have focus and intention and be in control, at least for men in dancing this is the case.

In France they use so called fixed steps drill or competition form, you dry to unbalance your opponent so that he or she touches the ground with other parts of the body but feet or that the back heel comes of the ground, or your feet moves sideways. It is a kind of fighting but many of the tai chi PH drills are more harmonious, at least in the beginning when you learn them.

This harmonious way of doing things makes it possible to research your own and your training partner's movement and cultivate the movement without hurrying and without the risk of injuries. Our bodies tend to tense under pressure, that can make learning of new things difficult or that you learn them wrongly from the beginning. Stress free environment makes it possible to learn proper, correct techniques and right body mechanics.

On a good foundation it is easy to build up more, new techniques, increase the speed, combine feet and hands, increase power etc.

In the next part of this book we take a closer look at some of the PH drills and what they contain. Keep in mind that often the more basic exercises are the most important ones and every drill can be done in many ways, for example increasing the complexity of the drill etc.

Single hand PH

Both trainees put their right foot on the same line, in a normal basic stance, we use back stance and front stance. One starts to push with the palm the other persons wrist, forcing him go to back stance and after that turn his waist and hips to redirect the force to the side.

Then you simply switch the roles, the defender becomes attacker and vice versa. In this style we use some resistance which is an excellent way to learn the whole body movement and timing with it and also it trains your hips and waist. Pay attention to your knees and feet, their right position is important both for health and to power leverage. Knees should be in a straight line over feet and should never exceed your toes. Your upper body should be controlled, not to lean in any direction. Even there is resistance, its level must not be too high, if the movement stops at some point it means that the pressure is too high and you should use less power.

Normally in this exercise we should not let the hand come to contact with the body but in Wudang tai chi we let it and continue pressure and the receiving part even bends his back to be able to take more power and the movement is redirected only shortly before the receiving part is losing the balance. In this way we study our own limits of balance and also our partners and also increase our ability. It is a quite heavy exercise done in this way but no pain, no gain.

I had difficulties in the beginning to practice in this way because it was against the principles, to let your hand to come into contact with your body and leaning heavily forward.

At this point I like this exercise a lot; I think you can gain a lot doing it properly. This is the hidden secret of martial arts, it is simple but you have to do your homework. People normally always want more and more advanced techniques but it is your basics that make you a master, or not.

Seven star steps

This exercise trains your footwork, mobility and what is the most important, to learn the right angles of attack and defense, in 45 degrees compared to your opponent. The pattern is easy, both move in 45 degrees angle for seven steps and then the roles change. Your hands are in contact with each other all the time. If you are redirecting the force you receive the opponent's hands with the outside on your palm on his wrist and inside of your palm on his elbow, thus controlling his arm and being easily able to handle any attack with that arm.

You can continue stepping more than seven steps if you are outside, you can continue to hundreds. Sometimes we decide that one is increasing the number of steps by one thus moving forward all the time, that is good when you have a limited space on your disposal.

The weight should be on one leg and you should be able to stop the movement without loosing your balance. There should be no delays and stops in the movement, if doing it right. Smooth changes of roles and continuity. We learn to attack in 45 degrees angle because then the outcome is not depending whose is stronger. We use normally this exercise for warming up, once I had to do it for several hours i London with advanced people. It was first after the seminar I realized that I had learned a lot. At that time I was thinking what was the point to pay the airline tickets to come and do the basic exercise.

I encourage my students to talk during the exercise; they should be able to do it so automatically that they can talk without doing mistakes.

PH drills can be made in many different ways, to increase the complexity and even speed. Seven star steps should not be done like single PH slowly, you can but when you comfortable you should do it with speed. Also can you vary speed and the length of steps, your training partner should be able to smoothly follow your changes. In the beginning it is better to have the same tempo and the lengt of steps should also be the same. Bow down, look up

This is an easy drill to learn but it is effective. I was discussing this exercise with my teacher about twenty years ago and he told me that this drill is one of them people tend to forget in their curriculum or it is left out because it is heavy to do.

Many of the basic drills are monotone and physically demanding but there, once again lies another secret. My Kung Fu teacher, Lawrence Leong used to say, "Kungfu is easy to learn but hard to master". The problem is, to quote my first Kali instructor, Hannu Hiltunen, people want to take the elevator to tenth floor, instead of working their way up.

Put your hands on your training partners shoulders and push, your partner should lean back maximally and when he or she cannot take it any more press down your hands and bow down, you keep the pressure on his body but so that he can hardly manage it. Not too much and not too little. Finally your hands touch his knees and the roles are switched.

It is a heavy exercise and teaches above many other things, how to lean away from blows and kicks, we cannot have a ideal controlled position of the body when dealing with self-defense. Even when we lean away we can defend ourselves with for example a kick.

This exercise trains your footwork, mobility and what is the most important, to learn the right angles of attack and defense, in 45 degrees compared to your opponent. The pattern is easy, both move in 45 degrees angle for seven steps and then the roles change. Your hands are in contact with each other all the time. If you are redirecting the force you receive the opponent's hands with the outside on your palm on his wrist and inside of your palm on his elbow, thus controlling his arm and being easily able to handle any attack with that arm.

You can continue stepping more than seven steps if you are outside, you can continue to hundreds. Sometimes we decide that one is increasing the number of steps by one thus moving forward all the time, that is good when you have a limited space on your disposal.

The weight should be on one leg and you should be able to stop the movement without loosing your balance. There should be no delays and stops in the movement, if doing it right. Smooth changes of roles and continuity. We learn to attack in 45 degrees angle because then the outcome is not depending whose is stronger. We use normally this exercise for warming up, once I had to do it for several hours i London with advanced people. It was first after the seminar I realized that I had learned a lot. At that time I was thinking what was the point to pay the airline tickets to come and do the basic exercise.

I encourage my students to talk during the exercise; they should be able to do it so automatically that they can talk without doing mistakes.

PH drills can be made in many different ways, to increase the complexity and even speed. Seven star steps should not be done like single PH slowly, you can but when you comfortable you should do it with speed.Also can you vary speed and the length of steps, your training partner should be able to smoothly follow your changes. In the beginning it is better to have the same tempo and the lengt of steps should also be the same.

Bow down, look up

This is an easy drill to learn but it is effective. I was discussing this exercise with my teacher about twenty years ago and he told me that this drill is one of them people tend to forget in their curriculum or it is left out because it is heavy to do.

Many of the basic drills are monotone and physically demanding but there, once again lies another secret. My Kung Fu teacher, Lawrence Leong used to say, "Kungfu is easy to learn but hard to master". The problem is, to quote my first Kali instructor, HannuHiltunen, people want to take the elevator to tenth floor, instead of working their way up.

Put your hands on your training partners shoulders and push, your partner should lean back maximally and when he or she cannot take it any more press down your hands and bow down, you keep the pressure on his body but so that he can hardly manage it. Not too much and not too little. Finally your hands touch his knees and the roles are switched.

It is a heavy exercise and teaches above many other things, how to lean away from blows and kicks, we cannot have a ideal controlled position of the body when dealing with self-defense. Even when we lean away we can defend ourselves with for example a kick.

Nine palace steps

In this drill you use stepping across, so that if left foot takes a step, right knee ends up near the left heel, knee does not touch the ground but can be close to floor. The toes of the crossing step foot points to your opponent, otherwise your power is not focused right. You take two cross steps forward and then two back stances where you redirect your opponents force to the side.

Four direction PH

40

This drill has derived its name straight from the tai chi theory. The active part is pushing (ji) your opponent straight to the chest with an open palm, the second push is directed downwards (an). The first push is redirected up and to the side (peng), and the second one is directed to the side and down (lu). In this drill you will learn later for example the use of spiraling power. It is well suited to train locks, sweeps, etc with a flow, you simply add techniques without your basic movement does not break or become not fluent.

Reelingsilk

Both hands has contact with your training partner o hands are circling inwards. From this basic movement you can choose to attack in the same tempo and without stops as if drawing a fragile silk, which can break and you should pay attention to a smooth and continuous movement. If our opponent is hindering our attack so we continue the movement once again and use circular movement to overcome our opponent.

Da Lu

The meaning of this book is not to teach PH but discuss. dalu is hard to explain. We use hexagrams all eight directions so that our footwork happens along the lines of hexagram or against them.

PH with feet.

I like to teach this drill because it improves ones balance very fast and is fun to do. Both practitioners have contact with their right feet and start to do a circular movement with their legs without losing contact. If you find this exercise difficult you can hold and get the support of your training partner. When you improve, start to make single hands pushing hands movement like taught in yang style. The hands looks like they are doing a circle but remember, one is pushing and the other person is redirect so it starts to look as if it is about circle they do, but they do pushing and redirecting. You can also try to do the circles in different directions if you can manage it.

After this is beginning to function you can start to kick the supporting leg of your partner, he in turn redirects the kick and maybe kick your leg and so on. Later you can try high kicks and you can attack with your hand in the same way as in reeling silk. In the end of day it is a kind of sparring, still not, where you can have fun, trying to be better than your partner. If it is too much raw power and struggle, refine your techniques instead of starting to wrestle.

The changes of direction PH

In every PH drill we use listening and sensitivity and it in its turn is possible only if we are relaxed and have a light contact with our opponent. This way we can sense or feel when our trainingspartner will change the direction of the drill. there should be no break in the movement and from outside you should not be able to observe anything else that the direction changed.

You should be able to do these changes whenever without any interruption in your drill.

The placement of hands in PH

Almost in every drill your hands are in contact with the other person's wrist and elbow. This is simply because in this way we can listen and control the opponents arm. By touching our opponent's wrist we can sense hitting with fist and by touching elbow, we can redirect elbow blows. We can also lock the arm, push it or pull it or break it. We can also control the arm with one arm and hit with the other.

Training blind folded

Training without seeing is good for sensing and the balance. Many PH practitioners tend to look away from their opponent; they use other senses than eyes. What comes to self-defense it is good to learn to use so called split vision or eagle vision, you look broadly and for example you have to see your opponents legs and arms at the same time because in self-defense we are not always in contact with our opponent.

How develop the skills needed in PH?

The best way to develop your skills in PH is to do the drills so that they become your second nature, it is also important to train with many different partners because everybody has differences and their strong and weak points. I think it is important to take it slow in the beginning and do your basic drills over and over again. PH is not a goal in itself; it is a tool/help that makes your self-defense more efficient by training certain skills and qualities which are needed. If your goal is to win PH competitions you should concentrate and train methods used in just competitions. I am not a great believer of specialization. In China already kids are being divided in certain groups, some train only tai chi forms, some only pushing hands and some fighting. With other words they are highly specialized already as children. I believe that by training all the aspects of tai chi chuan you can become good even in PH. It means Nei Kung training, hand form, weapon forms, self-defense etc. This kind of training is also good for the body and mind. Specialization means that the art becomes smaller, it is more boring to train and not necessary good for your health. In tai chi chuan you should develop all the aspects and not to forget good balance, both physically and mentally. If you want to compete can you have more the type of training you need in the competition. Maybe have an extra physical program made only for you, so you do not train too much or too little. It is important to remember to rest and have some periodicity in your training. I know personally a man who became one of the strongest men in the world, by cutting down his training by 50 percent. He was over trained all the time and results did not come.

One of my good friends has been competing a lot with success but he always trained his art as a whole art, not neglecting anything. He has won the most competitions but if he had only been preparing for competitions, who knows how far he could have gone. His choice was not to sacrifice his art on the altar of competition.

Many who compete in martial art stop completely training after they stop competing. This can be partly depending on that their skills on other fields than just where they were competing in, had not been developing since many years , of course, the lack of adrenalin kick is usually an important reason. There is a lot to be done with athletes who stop competing, quite many get different kinds of problems which should be taken seriously and there should be program and advice how to stop competing in a good way.

Different PH competition rules

It is quite natural to go over and describe PH competition rules after reasoning above. It is up to the reader to make an opinion about PH competitions but they are likewise a social fact as suicide is, whether we like it or not, they do exist. It was somewhat the same thing with the fact Emil Durkheim "invented". He came to this new idea that suicide is a social fact; it was a new thing but true.

It is also true that whether we like it or not competitions are a social fact, they exist. I make a very short, brief describing of the different rules or formats of competition. The rules are made by a man and can be changed but these rules, in general, are giving everybody the same equal chances to compete so my guess is that these rules will rule still some time in the future.

Fixed steps PH

As you can detach from its name, there is no footwork in fixed steps. You are not allowed to move your feet except lift the front foots toes up. Otherwise the feet have to be on the floor and are not allowed to glide in any direction or lifted up. You have contact with your opponent; both are touching each other's elbow and wrist. The referee keeps his hand on top and contestants make a circular motion with their hands. Then the referee shoots, fight and you are allowed to push and pull by the hands or push the body but not below waist and neck and face area. We do not go in to details on how you count the points but everybody can see who is winning, because you change the front foot every time somebody gets a point, of course if you touch the floor with other parts than feet your opponent will get more points etc but except from some foot faults you do not have to be expert to see who is winning. In my mind these rules are clear and easy to follow for everybody. This type of PH is taking place in the big tai chi happenings all over Europe, so it is used in other contexts as well.

Restricted steps

If I remember right this competition form was invented in Holland and was called Dutch PH before. Anyway, in this competition your front feet should stay inside a marked circle but you can move freely around with the back leg. The idea should be same here, to use evasion and not only confront your opponent. Naturally with these rules weight differences play a more important role. You should not lose yourself and your techniques in this format. It is only to continue to apply tai chi principles even if it is harder to do than for example in fixed steps. It is also a good idea that sometimes to move and lose a point because with these rules your knees can end up in strange positions and if you are stubborn, you maybe will damage your knee. The risk to get an injury is when you have actually lost a point but continue fighting in a bad position, think about it. You also loose energy by struggling in a situation that is bad for you, so sometimes it is better to retreat in order to win later. In my mind all these competition formats should be used in ordinary training, maybe not right away but they are excellent methods to improve many things, also the most important one, listening. When you are under a pressure you tend to forget everything, so practice with so many different people as possible, even with different seizes and levels. The best opponent is much bigger than you and on a higher level in PH than you are. This was the way William C. C. Chen told us he had become so good in listening. He started to train with older guys and much heavier and more powerful than him. The only way for him was to listen and neutralize

Moving steps

Here the forbidden things are few and allowed things many. You can move freely on a area 4*4 meter, you can sweep, throw, lock, push pull etc. If you throw somebody and follow uncontrolled on the floor you will not get points, you can't even touch the ground with other parts than your feet. You try to lock your opponent, push him away from the area or get him down in the mat.

It is very demanding physically and you can often see matches where the one who has been better the first part of the match, loses because he or she did not have enough stamina. This is very close to wrestling, although tai chi does not prefer wrestling techniques because we always count on several opponents and start to wrestle with one is a suicide. Then it happens in a fight, very easily, that we end up in wrestling. Do not mix PH with self-defense. Even though I won against much younger opponents in Birmingham I was not thinking that I could win over these young and fit, hard training tai chi brothers in a fight, not in a competition or in a street but I was still proud to win:-).

Remember that PH is tool in self-defense.

I have to say that the people organizing the competition were gentlemen. It was a surprise that they congratulated me warmly. This should be the spirit in competition, if it is, I am sure I am not against them.
I can now, after so many years, tell about the strange way I was brought up. I got no money if I won a competition but I earned the more money the worse I did. I think the idea being was that sports are good for you but not competitions, at least so I interpret it.

I think you should not take the sword from the boys, as a good friend put it. It is good to test your capability in a controlled environment, they test it anyway and otherwise they end up testing it in the streets with motorcycles, cars and with each other.

The biggest risk with competition in PH is that you start to consider PH as important in itself, it becomes an end. It is important in the tai chi chuan system but it is only a part in a bigger picture and a tool, as we have mentioned now quite many times. It is normally needed a very short   time.
Below I will help the reader to see different levels that PH can be seen, depending on the focus, how close look we take. We start from a more abstract level and then start focus more and more.

Analysis and conclusions, the three different levels in PH

Level 1

On this level we cannot see any details, we can only understand that we might have some use of PH drills, it helps us to defend ourselves.

Level 2

Now we can see that PH helps us to improve our mobility, footwork, timing, distance etc. We could continue with better posture, balance, whole body force etc. All these things are improving when we practice PH.

Level 3

Now we take a very close look what is really happening under a very short time in PH. We are in contact with our opponent, we are relaxed and soft and we can listen to our opponents force and redirect it after that we can use an appropriate technique depending on the situation. We maybe are happy with redirecting the force, our friend wanted to test us after too many drinks or we can pull, push, strike, kick, throw, break, strangle and lock depending how threatening the situation is. To summarize: PH drills and skills are needed a very short, limited time but it can decide the outcome in self-defense situation!

Why to train

There are plenty of reasons why a tai chi practitioner should train PH and all of them have not to do with martial side. You learn also body mechanics, relaxation and right body and feet positions. One American tai chi teacher told in his book that he and his wife use it to solve problems, they do PH and discuss. You can have a poker face but body tenses if you lie so they use PH in pair therapy purposes. I do not think that it is wrong to use PH like this and develop methods to apply PH but I do not think that you should call them tai chi anymore. It is question of something new that has been inspired by the art of tai chi.

Don't make PH to a goal in itself, I think it is an intelligent and fun way to train important things needed in tai chi chuan.

Everybody can do it on some level and the good news are that the more you practice, the better you will be. I think the most rewarding and interesting thing is that you can explore research movement together with somebody else. You maybe do not discover new things everyday but you have to have fun every time, otherwise it is not going to last the rest of your lifetime. There are pits and parts in tai chi training that are not so great fun but good for you so spare PH for fun. I wish all the practitioners pleasant moments doing tai chi pushing hands.

Thanks

Sanna Manninen has been an invaluable help in the process of writing this book. Thank You for all the help, it was great to have you on my side.

Thanks to Johan and Tommi for your time and encouraging words, they are needed in this cold world:-).

Thank You JKD.fi for lending your training place for photos.

Thank You Ville and Timo for being helpful taking pics and acting as photo models.

Thank You Anne for taking photos in Sunstrand in Helsinki.

Other photos: Sophie Nyrell has taken the two pics from Tai chi Chuan EM 2008. Thanks Mattias Nyrell helping me getting those pics.

In the photos that show a staff as a training aid it is only a question of a warming up, avoiding exercise. You cannot take steps but have to turn your body, jump or kneel. In the beginning you can use a soft weapon and then a wooden one as in the picture.

© 2014 Heikki Nousiainen
Kustantaja: BoD – Books on Demand, Helsinki, Suomi
Valmistaja: BoD – Books on Demand, Norderstedt, Saksa
ISBN: 978-952-318-403-9